Of All the Words I Never Said

By
Hurrera Khan

All Rights Reserved
Copyright © 2025 Hurrera Khan

ISBN - 978-1-5356-0197-9

ISBN - 978-1-5356-0198-6

All rights reserved. No part of this publication may be reproduced, distributed, or transmitted in any form or by any means without the prior written permission of the author.

Table of Contents

Author's Note i
Dedication ii
Introduction Before the First Word iii
Chapter 1: The First Word I Swallowed 1
Chapter 2: Where the Voice Broke 4
Chapter 3: Eyes That Asked, Lips That Didn't Answer ... 8
Chapter 4: Loving Quietly, Losing Loudly 12
Chapter 5: A Letter I Never Sent 15
Chapter 6: The Weight of Almost 18
Chapter 7: The Places Where You Still Exist 22
Chapter 8: The Things I Left Unsaid 25
Chapter 9: What It Taught Me About Love 28
Chapter 10: When You Miss Someone Who's Still Alive 32
Chapter 11: What I Learned in the Quiet 36
Chapter 12: I Loved You Gently 39
Chapter 13: The Versions of You I Still Carry 42
Chapter 14: The Art of Letting Go Without Closure 45
Chapter 15: The Day I Stopped Waiting 49
Chapter 16: The Way I Love Now 53

Chapter 17: How I Forgave You (Even Without an Apology) 58

Chapter 18: The Kind of Love I Deserve 63

Chapter 19: If You Ever Think of Me Again 67

Chapter 20: The Things I Never Said Aloud 71

Chapter 21: The Silence I Needed to Hear 75

Chapter 22: What I Know About Love Now 79

Chapter 23: I Don't Miss You Anymore 83

Chapter 24: If We Had Met at a Different Time 86

Chapter 25: I Still Carry You in Small Ways 90

Chapter 26: I Needed to Lose You to Find Myself 94

Chapter 27: Some Goodbyes Aren't Loud 98

Chapter 28: Some Things Don't Deserve a Second Chance 102

Chapter 29: It Didn't End with You, It Began with Me 106

Chapter 30: Of All the Words I Never Said 109

Author's Note

This book was never meant to be loud.

It was meant to feel like someone sitting next to you in the quiet, someone who knows the weight of unspoken things.

These pages hold moments I never had the courage to voice, the ache I once mistook for love, and the parts of myself I had to lose just to find. If you saw yourself in these words, in the pauses, in the stillness, in the letting go then maybe this wasn't just my story after all.

Maybe it was ours.

And maybe, just maybe, the words you've never said...

will find their voice one day too.

Until then

be gentle with your heart.

It remembers everything

you're still trying to forget.

The one who finally spoke

Dedication

For the ones who loved quietly.

Who stayed longer than they should have.

Who broke silently and healed slowly.

For the hearts full of words they never got to say

this book is yours.

You were never weak for feeling deeply.

You were always enough, even in your silence.

Introduction
Before the First Word

There are things I should have said when your name was still soft in my mouth.

Things I wanted to scream into the night sky, but only managed to bury in my chest.

This book is not a story.

It's a collection of silences.

Every page is a breath I held, a feeling I swallowed, a goodbye I rehearsed but never gave.

For the ones who loved quietly.

For the ones who broke privately.

For the ones who are still carrying letters that never found an address—

this is for you.

Because maybe some words were never meant to be spoken.

They were meant to be felt.

Chapter 1: The First Word I Swallowed

It began in a moment that didn't look important, just another day, just another quiet corner. Nothing dramatic. No music swelling in the background, no sky falling. And yet, something in that moment held the weight of everything that could have changed my life. We were sitting beside each other, not touching, not speaking much, just quietly existing in the same space. But even in the silence, something between us felt like it mattered. There was a softness in the air, a closeness that wasn't defined by words. I felt it. Deeply. And somewhere inside, I knew, I wanted to say something. Not a grand confession. Just something small and honest enough to shift the space between us. Something like, "I like being near you." Or, "You feel like home."

But I didn't. I said nothing. I looked away when I should've looked closer. I swallowed the words, as I had done many times before, burying them beneath my ribs as if silence could protect me. I don't even know why I held back. Maybe it was fear of being seen. Maybe it was pride. Or maybe I believed that speaking the truth might change what was safe, and at that time, silence still felt safer than rejection.

I had been taught to be strong, and somewhere along the way, I misunderstood strength as silence. I convinced myself that not speaking was maturity. That holding back was wise. That feelings, when unspoken, became easier to manage. But that wasn't true. They only grew louder in the quiet. I remember a day, late afternoon, light pouring through a window like forgiveness, when you laughed at something I said, and then looked at me like I mattered. My heart nearly gave itself away in that instant. I could feel the words building up inside me, desperate to escape. But all I did was smile, pretend it was just another moment. And just like that, the truth passed me by.

Later, when I saw you with someone else, I smiled again. Because that's what I've always done, carry pain without making a sound. You asked if I was okay. I said, "Of course." But inside, I was unraveling. What I wanted to say was, "No. I'm not okay. I thought maybe you were meant to stay." But the moment passed, and I let it. Again.

That was the first word I swallowed. It wasn't just a word. It was a door I never opened. And sometimes, even now, I still stand in front of that closed door in my mind and wonder what might've been different if I had spoken. Maybe it wouldn't have changed anything. Maybe it would've hurt. But at least I wouldn't have been haunted by the silence.

Silence can become a habit. At first, it's a choice. Then, a language. Then, a weight. I carried that weight into every space I entered after you, into other conversations, other hearts, other possibilities. And every time I almost spoke my truth again, I remembered what it felt like to be silent the first time. I remembered the cost.

So if you're reading this and you're holding something in, something real, something honest, something buried, this is what I need to tell you, some words may hurt when spoken, but they hurt more when they live inside you, unanswered. I don't know if it would've made a difference that day if I had said something. But I know this, I should have. And I'm sorry I didn't.

Chapter 2: Where the Voice Broke

There are moments you never forget, not because they were loud or grand, but because they held something sacred you couldn't hold onto. I remember that day so clearly. The air was heavy, like it knew something I didn't. I stood in front of you, heart racing, words clawing at the back of my throat. I had practiced it all in my head, what I would say, how I would say it, how I wouldn't let my voice tremble. But when the moment finally came, everything inside me fell silent.

You were talking, laughing maybe, I don't even remember the words. My mind was too loud with everything I hadn't said for weeks. I looked at you, and for a second, I thought I saw something in your eyes. A softness. A stillness. An opening. It was my chance. My one fragile chance. And I let it slip. Again.

I opened my mouth to speak, but the voice broke before it could form. Not from weakness, not entirely. But from the sheer weight of what had been left unsaid for so long. I had held back so many truths for so many days that now they had become strangers to my tongue. I was no longer fluent in my own emotions. The words didn't come. Only silence did. And you looked at me, waiting, just for a breath. Just for a flicker of something real. And I gave you a smile instead.

I've never forgiven myself for that smile. It was the lie I wore so often it became my skin. You didn't see the storm behind it. How could you? I had spent so long becoming invisible in front of the person I wanted to see me the most. I had mistaken quiet for dignity. I had convinced myself that the ache of staying silent was better than the risk of being misunderstood.

But what I didn't realize is that silence can be just as loud as rejection. That not saying what you feel doesn't save you from heartbreak, it becomes the heartbreak. That day, you asked me something casual. Something small. I could've answered with the truth, but I softened it, filtered it, gave you something lighter than what I carried. And I watched you nod, unaware of the storm inside me. That moment passed like so many others, unspoken, unfinished, unresolved. But for me, it never left.

It stayed in the corners of my thoughts, replayed in long walks home, in songs I couldn't listen to anymore, in the pages of empty journals. I would go back to that moment over and over again, asking myself the same question, Why didn't I say it? The answer was never clear. Maybe I thought the words would ruin what little closeness we had. Maybe I thought you already knew and didn't care. Or maybe I didn't think I was worth hearing. That last one hurt the most.

The truth is, I had spent so long hiding parts of myself, I didn't know how to reveal them anymore. I wasn't just silent with you, I was silent with myself. I avoided mirrors. Avoided feelings. Avoided confronting the parts of me that ached to be acknowledged. And by the time I realized I had something worth saying, the silence had already settled like dust on everything.

Sometimes I wonder if you ever sensed it. If you ever paused and thought, He's holding something back. Maybe you did. Maybe you didn't. All I know is, I stood in front of someone who once made the world feel less heavy, and I couldn't even say "Please don't go." The voice broke before the words did.

After you left, I stood there alone, trying to catch my breath. I remember how quiet everything felt. Like the world itself had stopped to mourn the sentence that never escaped my mouth. I wanted to run after you. I wanted to say it anyway. But pride is a quiet killer. And I had already swallowed enough for a lifetime.

That night, I didn't sleep. I lay awake thinking about how strange it is that we can spend our whole lives with people and never really speak to them. That we can laugh together, sit shoulder to shoulder, even love them silently, and still leave them never knowing who we truly were. That's the curse of silence. It doesn't just hide your truth; it hides you.

The next day, everything returned to normal. But I didn't. I carried that unspoken moment like a scar no one could see. And over time, it became easier to pretend it never happened. To act like I never tried. Like I never felt what I did. But the truth? I did try. Even if the words never came. Even if the voice broke. I tried.

And maybe that's what hurts the most, not that I failed to speak, but that I let fear define who I was in front of the one person I wanted to be fully honest with.

I've learned since then that we don't get endless chances. That some moments only come once, and when they pass, they don't return. You don't always get another try. You don't always get to rewrite the scene. Sometimes, the only thing you get is a memory, and the ache of all the words you never said.

Chapter 3: Eyes That Asked, Lips That Didn't Answer

There's a kind of silence that isn't quiet, the kind that holds too much, says too much, without speaking a word. I saw that silence in your eyes once. More than once. It was there in the way you looked at me when we sat across from each other, the world carrying on in the background, but something between us stayed still. Your eyes asked questions you never voiced, and I gave you answers I never spoke. That was how we existed, in this unspoken space, two people talking without sound, hoping the other would be brave enough to say it first.

I used to think if someone looked at you long enough, deeply enough, they'd understand you, that words wouldn't be necessary. But the truth is, they are. Eyes may speak, but they can also lie. They can ask without ever truly waiting for an answer. They can pretend to be brave and still hide behind fear. And that's what we both did. We watched each other closely, but neither of us truly saw the other clearly. Or maybe we did, and just didn't know what to do with what we saw.

There was a moment, just one, that still lives in my memory like it happened yesterday. We were sitting side by side, shoulders barely touching. The air between us felt charged, but still tender. You looked at me, not like before, but with something heavier, like a question you'd rehearsed a thousand times but couldn't say. I met your gaze for a second too long. I knew what you wanted. You wanted me to say something real. To admit what we both felt but neither of us named. But I didn't. I looked away. I smiled. I gave you comfort instead of truth. And in doing so, I think I let you go, without ever truly having you.

Later, when I was alone, I realized how many conversations we had that way, without words. Entire exchanges made of glances and silences, hope wrapped in hesitation. That's how you can lose someone you never held by waiting too long to answer a question they never dared to ask. And it's strange, how much meaning one moment can carry. How it stays with you longer than all the ones that followed.

I think about you when I see other eyes now, when I meet people who are good at pretending they don't feel too much. I've become one of them. I've learned to master small talk. I've learned how to talk about everything except what matters. Because once you've let something true slip through your fingers, you start to doubt whether you're still capable of holding anything real again.

I wonder sometimes what would've happened if I had reached for your hand that day. If I had said something as simple as "I know what you're asking." But I didn't. I let your eyes keep asking, and I let mine answer with silence. And the truth is, I was scared. Not of rejection, not even of heartbreak. I was scared of being known. Of being fully seen, and still left behind. And maybe you were scared too.

And here, in the quiet of reflection,

a small poem finds its way in:

Your eyes held a question

my lips were too afraid to meet.

So we danced in almosts

and lived in incomplete.

We never spoke the language

our hearts were fluent in

and maybe that's why

we never truly began.

Now, I've come to understand that not all connections are broken by arguments or distance. Some fall apart because two people stood too close to the truth and turned away. We both did that. And it doesn't make either of us wrong. Just unfinished.

Some people look back on relationships and remember the laughter. I remember the silence. The way your eyes held more than your words ever did. The way my lips never found the courage to answer. And that's what lingers, not what we said, but what we didn't. The moment passed, and with it, everything that might have been. And still, in the middle of crowded rooms, I sometimes feel like I see you. Not physically, but in the way someone tilts their head when they're listening, in the way they laugh a second too late, in the way their eyes seem to be carrying something they'll never speak of.

In those moments, I remember you again. And I remember myself, the boy who sat beside someone he couldn't stop thinking about, and chose to smile instead of speak. I'm still learning how to forgive him.

Chapter 4: Loving Quietly, Losing Loudly

There are kinds of love that never get to breathe in the open air, love that lives in the pauses between texts, in the way you remember someone when there's nothing left to hold. It's the kind of love that sits across from you, laughs with you, walks beside you, and yet never truly knows how much of your heart it holds. That was the kind of love I gave. It was quiet, careful, careful enough not to break the moment, careful enough not to risk the comfort of being near you, even if never truly with you. It wasn't love at first sight. It was love in long silences, in subtle glances, in the soft ache of not saying too much. I didn't confess it in grand words. I didn't show up in the rain with open arms. I just kept showing up in your life, hoping that somewhere in my presence, you'd feel my absence before it ever arrived. But I was mistaken. Because sometimes people don't notice what they have until it no longer waits quietly in the background. And sometimes, silence becomes too heavy to carry, even for someone who's mastered it. You started pulling away, and I felt it before you ever said it. That's the cruelty of quiet love, it notices everything but still says nothing.

I watched you become distant. I watched your replies get shorter. I watched you laugh louder with someone else. And even then, I said nothing.

Then one day, you were gone. No fight. No reason. Just absence, loud, aching, final. That's when I realized something I hadn't been ready to face: the person who loves silently suffers the loudest. Because there's no story to explain the grief. No memories to point to. No "us" to defend. Just a heart broken by something that never had a name. And in that quiet mourning, Faiz's words came to me, not as verses, but as truth, as understanding.

"My heart, my lost child, where have you wandered?

There was no sorrow in our parting.

Only silence, and the rustle of your absence.

If this is love, it is not written in declarations.

It is written in waiting, in what is left behind."

"Don't ask me for the love I once gave you.

I had thought that life would be nothing but your light, your warmth.

But there are other griefs in the world.

Other joys too."

I didn't understand those words before. I do now. They speak the language of the quiet-hearted, those of us who loved with restraint and lost without noise. I still think about you sometimes. Not out of longing. Not out of regret. But because your absence taught me more than your presence ever could. I learned that loving someone quietly doesn't mean you didn't love them fully. It means you loved them with reverence, with patience, with fear, fear of losing them, fear of speaking too soon, fear of being too much. And in the end, that fear came true anyway. If I had another chance, would I say something? Would I risk everything just to hear how it might have ended? I still don't know. What I do know is that some stories don't need a final chapter to be remembered. Some loves don't need to be understood to have mattered. And some hearts, even after breaking, still carry the echo of someone else's name. That's the kind of love I gave, quiet while it lived, and loud when it died.

Chapter 5:
A Letter I Never Sent

I don't know what made me pick up a pen today. Maybe it's the weight of the silence you left behind. Or maybe it's because every time I try to move on, I find myself returning to you, not in body, but in memory, in questions I never asked, and answers I never gave.

This isn't a confession. It's not even an apology. It's just... everything I never said when I had the chance.

If you ever wondered how I felt, truly felt, the truth is, I loved you. Not in a way that needed announcements or declarations, but in the kind of way that makes ordinary moments feel sacred. I loved you in the way I paid attention to things no one else noticed. I loved you in silence, painfully, patiently, and fully.

I was afraid, more than anything else. Afraid that if I said the words, I'd lose you. That if I opened my heart, the air would shift and whatever closeness we had would vanish. So I stayed quiet. I laughed when I wanted to cry. I stood still when I wanted to reach for you. I pretended to be okay with "just being there" when all I really wanted was to be chosen. I told myself my love was safer in the background, but the truth is, it was slowly dying there.

You probably never knew how much I noticed. How I watched you fade. How I felt your warmth grow colder. How I stayed up nights wondering if I had imagined all of it. And when you left, not with anger, not even with closure, but just with silence, I didn't chase you. I didn't ask you to stay. But only because I didn't think I had the right to.

You see, we never had a moment. We had moments. A thousand almosts. A hundred quiet promises we never put into words. That's what made losing you so complicated. There was no ending, only the sound of something unfinished closing itself quietly. And maybe that's why I'm still writing this. To find a place for all the words that had no place back then.

Sometimes, I wonder what would have happened if I had just told you. If I had looked you in the eyes and said, "I love you, and I don't know how to carry it quietly anymore." Maybe it would've changed everything. Or maybe nothing at all. But at least I wouldn't have had to write this now, alone, late at night, to someone who will never read it.

You were not a chapter in my life. You were a language I didn't know how to speak. And by the time I learned it, there was no one left to hear me.

If this letter ever found you, and it won't, I hope you'd understand. I hope you'd see that I didn't hold back because I didn't feel enough. I held back because I felt too much. I wasn't silent because I didn't care, I was silent because I cared so deeply that it scared me.

And now, I write this not for you, but for the part of me that still aches for what I never allowed myself to say.

Maybe this letter is just an ending I had to give myself,

because I never got one from you.

But even now, after all the distance,

after all the silence,

after all the healing I pretend I've done,

if you ever asked me,

"Did you love me?"

I'd still answer,

Always.

Even now.

Chapter 6: The Weight of Almost

Sometimes I think the heaviest things we carry aren't the memories of what happened, but the shadows of what almost did.

There's a strange ache in moments that almost became something. You remember them not as stories, but as possibilities you still feel in your chest. You walk through the world pretending you're over it, but every once in a while, something reminds you, a song, a time of day, a quiet street, and suddenly, you're standing at the edge of a moment that once begged to mean more.

I had many of those with you.

The moment your hand brushed mine and stayed just long enough to ask a question my lips were too afraid to answer. The time your eyes lingered a second too long, and I wondered if you were hoping I'd say something, anything. Or that one night when we sat in silence, both knowing there was something unspoken rising in the room between us, and neither of us reached for it.

We were always close to something. Close to clarity. Close to honesty. Close to being more. But we never crossed that invisible line. We always stopped at almost.

And "almost" has a way of digging itself into your memory like it owns the place. It doesn't let you forget. It leaves questions without endings and goodbyes without good. It doesn't break like heartbreak does. It just... stays.

There were so many things I wanted to tell you. Things I had rehearsed a hundred times in my head but never once aloud. I wanted to tell you that you made me feel safe, not in the way a shelter does, but in the way a sky does. Quietly. Vastly. Unapologetically. That even when we said nothing, I felt seen. That even when we joked, I felt the weight of what we weren't saying underneath. That I looked at you and thought, If anything in this world ever felt right, it was this, even in silence.

But I told myself it wasn't the right time. And then the time passed.

It always does.

You drifted away, slowly, naturally, the way unspoken things do. And I let you. Not because I didn't care, but because I didn't know how to stop someone who was never really mine. I convinced myself that you knew how I felt. That you must have seen it. That maybe, just maybe, you chose to ignore it because you didn't feel the same. And maybe you didn't. Or maybe you were just like me, scared, unsure, waiting for a sign that never came.

We were two people circling around something beautiful, but neither of us dared to touch it. So now all I have are the remnants of closeness, the softness of what could have been, and the constant hum of "what if."

I don't talk about you anymore. Not because I've forgotten, but because no one ever understands how something that never happened can still feel like a loss. But it was. And it is. You were a quiet kind of loss, the kind that didn't rip anything apart, but still left something missing.

And yet, I've come to accept that not everything unfinished is a tragedy. Some stories are meant to stay open-ended. Some feelings are meant to be lived in silence. And some people are meant to teach you how deeply you can feel… even when nothing ever truly begins.

You were my almost. My unanswered question. My paused breath. And even now, long after we've drifted into separate lives, I still carry the weight of you, not as a regret, but as a truth I once lived quietly.

You weren't a mistake.

You were a moment.

A soft one.

A near one.

A heavy one.

One I'll never quite put down.

Chapter 7:
The Places Where You Still Exist

You don't live in my life anymore. Not in the way that matters to the world, not in phone calls, not in messages, not in plans. But somehow, you still exist in the quiet spaces where no one else can see you.

You're in the song that plays late at night when I'm not even paying attention, but my heart tightens anyway. You're in the way I take my coffee now, not because you taught me, but because I learned to like the kind you used to sip, just to feel a little closer to the time when we sat together, saying everything and nothing.

I find you in places I don't expect. In bookstores, in sentences, in strangers who turn their heads the same way you used to when you were listening carefully. Sometimes you're in the early morning sky, calm, dim, and vast, like something just out of reach. Other times you're in a scent that passes by in a crowd and hits me like a memory I didn't know I still remembered.

You've become a part of my map, not in red lines or marked destinations, but in unspoken detours. There are corners of this city

I avoid, not because they hurt, but because they hold too much. They carry your laugh, your silence, your ghost. And I've learned that grief isn't just a feeling. It's a geography. It lives in spaces. It attaches itself to doors I no longer open, songs I can't finish, streets I walk a little faster down.

I still see you in the things I don't talk about. In the way I hesitate when someone new asks me what I'm looking for. In the pause before I answer. In the fact that I often don't.

You don't live in my days anymore, but you show up in my pauses, in the spaces between moments. When I'm quiet. When I'm tired. When the world slows down just enough to let the memory of you catch up.

And sometimes, it's not sadness. Sometimes, it's just recognition, like running your fingers across a scar and remembering how it healed. You don't bleed anymore, but you remember the pain. And in some strange way, you honor it.

I think some people don't fade. They just... relocate. From your life to your memory. From the front of your mind to the corners of it. And you carry them, not because you want to, but because they became part of your wiring, a line in your story that you can't erase without losing something true.

You exist now in the way I love differently. More carefully. A little quieter. With more attention to all the things I once ignored. You taught me that. Without knowing, without trying. You changed the way I see the world. And even though you're gone, you're still here, in the small, ordinary places that remember you when I try not to.

Chapter 8:
The Things I Left Unsaid

There are conversations that live inside your chest long after the person is gone. Words that never found their way into air. Things you rehearsed in your mind a hundred times but always swallowed at the edge of your lips. I used to think silence was gentle. That it protected both people. But I've learned now, it doesn't protect, it delays. It builds a storm inside you. And one day, it starts to rain.

I still carry all the things I never told you. Not the dramatic confessions, not the tearful breakdowns, just the soft truths. The kind of things that sound small, but meant everything. I wanted to tell you that your presence changed me. That just the sound of your voice on a dull day made me feel like I could breathe again. That being near you felt like finding something I wasn't even looking for. That I noticed the way your eyes lit up when you were talking about something you loved. That sometimes I stayed quiet just to hear you speak a little longer.

I wanted to tell you I was scared. That loving you quietly was breaking me loudly. That every time I held back, I wasn't being strong, I was hurting. But I didn't want to burden you. I didn't want to risk losing you. So I let the silence do the talking, hoping it would be enough. It wasn't.

There were texts I typed and never sent. Drafts I deleted at 2am. Voice notes I recorded and never played. And moments where I stood in front of you, heartbeat wild in my chest, and still said nothing.

Maybe I thought the words would find their way eventually. That we had time. That if something was real enough, it didn't need to be spoken. But time isn't patient with silence. It doesn't wait for you to be ready. It moves. And if you don't speak, someone else will.

And they did.

You left without ever knowing the full weight of what I felt. Without hearing the things I'd been dying to say. And the worst part? I had so many chances. So many windows. And I closed them all.

There are letters I never wrote,

and sentences that ended inside me.

There are goodbyes I never gave,

because I was still hoping you'd stay.

There are words, soft, fragile, honest

that still sit heavy in my chest,

whispering what I was too afraid to speak.

People ask me if I ever told you. I shake my head and say, "No, it didn't feel like the right time." But the truth is, I was just afraid the right time would never come, and I didn't want to hear you say you didn't feel the same. So I chose silence. And silence, I've learned, is its own kind of answer.

Now, I find myself talking to memories. I still say those words, just not to you. I whisper them in the dark. I write them in notebooks. I release them into the pages of a story no one will know is yours. It's strange, how something can remain unsaid, but still shape your life completely.

You were never mine. But the things I didn't say? They still belong to me. And maybe that's the most honest kind of grief, knowing you never got to tell your truth. Knowing the echo inside you never became a voice in the world. It just stayed there, lingering, waiting, unfinished.

So here's the truth, now, long after it could change anything, I loved you. Not with fireworks or fairy tales, but with real, quiet feeling. I loved you in moments you probably didn't even notice. I loved you enough to stay. I loved you too much to speak.

And maybe that's where we ended, in the things I left unsaid.

Chapter 9: What It Taught Me About Love

People say heartbreak teaches you about pain. That once you lose someone you deeply care for, you learn how much the human heart can carry before it breaks. And while that's true, it's not the whole truth. What I learned from losing you wasn't just about pain, it was about love itself. Real love. The kind no one teaches you how to survive when it doesn't return the way you gave it.

Loving you quietly, and losing you even more quietly, rewrote everything I thought I understood about what love was supposed to be. I used to think love needed big moments, grand gestures, dramatic declarations, fireworks and timing that made sense. I believed love was something loud. But you showed me that love can be small and still be everything. It can be hidden in long walks, in the way someone listens, in staying when it's easier to walk away. Love, I learned, isn't always loud. Sometimes it's a presence. Sometimes it's just being seen, even when no words are spoken.

But here's what else I learned: love must be brave. And silence, no matter how noble it feels, is not love's friend. I kept mine wrapped in caution and what-ifs. I protected my heart so carefully that I forgot love isn't meant to be locked away. It's meant to breathe. It's meant to speak. I was so afraid of losing you that I never gave you a chance to choose me. I let fear dress up as patience. I mistook silence for strength. I thought that loving you from a distance, in quiet loyalty, was enough.

It wasn't.

And maybe that's the greatest lesson, love, to be real, must risk. It must open its chest and say, This is me. This is what I feel. I don't know what happens next, but I can't pretend I don't care. That's what I should've done. And now that you're gone, I carry that lesson like a mirror: painful to look into, but honest.

I also learned that love is not a contract. It doesn't guarantee anything. Just because you give it purely, doesn't mean it will be returned the same. You can love someone with everything you have, and they can still walk away. That used to feel unfair. But now, it feels human. No one owes us their heart. That's what makes it precious when it's given freely.

More than anything, I learned that love reveals you to yourself. After you left, I didn't just grieve you, I met myself. I met the parts of me I ignored when I was loving you. The insecurities

I buried, the needs I silenced, the dreams I delayed. I realized how much of myself I had poured into the idea of us, and how little I had kept for me. And so, slowly, I began to rebuild.

Not with bitterness, but with clarity. I forgave myself for the silence. I forgave you for not staying. I stopped wishing things were different, and started asking what I could do with what was left. That's what love, even the kind that ends, should do. It should leave you better. Softer, not harder. Wiser, not colder.

I know now that real love doesn't always last, but it always leaves something behind. A shift. A lesson. A way of seeing the world more honestly. You taught me that I want to be with someone who speaks, who shows, who stays. Someone who chooses openly, not out of convenience, not out of comfort, but out of courage.

You taught me what love isn't. And in doing so, you showed me what it must be.

Love is not a secret to be hoarded.

It is a truth to be shared.

It is not a quiet ache hidden in the chest,

it is a voice that trembles but speaks anyway.

Love is not about waiting for the right time

it's about creating the moment

before it passes you forever.

One day, I'll love again. But not the way I loved you, not quietly, not fearfully. Next time, I'll love with both hands open. I'll say the words when I feel them. I'll stay where I'm wanted, and I'll leave where I'm not. Because I've learned that silence doesn't protect love, it buries it.

And I won't bury anything ever again.

Chapter 10: When You Miss Someone Who's Still Alive

There's a strange kind of sadness that comes from missing someone who's still alive. Someone who walks through the world, laughs at things, lives their days, while you sit quietly in a corner of your own life, aching for a presence that used to be part of yours. There's no closure. No final words. Just a slow fading. A growing silence where there used to be warmth.

You don't realize how hard it is at first. You think maybe they're just busy. Maybe things will return to normal soon. You hold on to the hope that it's temporary, that something this real couldn't just disappear. But days pass. Then weeks. And slowly, you begin to accept the unspoken truth: they're not coming back. Not in the way they used to. Not to the version of you that remembers what it felt like to matter to them.

And yet… they're still here. Somewhere. Laughing. Talking. Living. They didn't leave the world. They just left your world. And that's what makes it so complicated. Because how do you grieve someone who didn't die? How do you mourn someone who could call you tomorrow, but won't?

There were so many times I picked up my phone, typed your name, stared at it, and put it away again. It felt too late to say something, and too early to pretend I was okay. I wondered if you ever thought of me, not out of guilt, but out of kindness. I wondered if anything ever reminded you of what we had, or if it's only me who walks through memories like they still belong to someone else.

And even though you're not here, you still live in the rhythm of my thoughts. I still turn around expecting to find you in certain conversations. I still imagine your voice when I'm sitting in places we used to talk. And that's the cruelest part, you're alive in the world, but absent from mine. Like a door I can see but no longer open.

There is no funeral for this kind of loss,

no ceremony for a goodbye that never came.

You just carry it,

the way shadows carry the shape of something

long after it's gone.

You mourn quietly,

at odd hours,

in unexpected places.

You miss them in the pause between thoughts,

in songs that never meant anything before,

and in smiles you wish they could still see.

People don't understand this kind of missing. They ask, "Why don't you just call?" Or worse, "Why are you still holding on?" As if presence can be requested. As if absence is always a choice. What they don't see is that it's not about pride. It's not even about pain. It's about honoring what was, and realizing what will never be again.

I've learned that just because someone is still breathing doesn't mean they haven't left. And just because you let go doesn't mean you stop feeling. You can carry love and distance at the same time. You can miss someone and still accept that they no longer belong in the story you're writing now.

Missing someone who's alive is a quiet kind of grief, one that asks for nothing, not even return. It just sits beside you in silence, like an old friend who knows not to speak. You don't want them back. You just want to remember without hurting. You want to smile when you think of them, instead of feeling like your chest forgot how to stay whole.

And slowly, you learn to do just that. You wake up one day and realize the memory no longer stings the same way. You pass by a familiar place and don't have to look away. You hear their name and it doesn't unravel you. That's when you know you haven't forgotten, you've just made peace.

You still miss them. But it's softer now. Less like a wound, more like a scar. Something you carry, but no longer bleed from.

Chapter 11: What I Learned in the Quiet

After you left, the world didn't shatter. It just slowed down. The days still came. The clocks still ticked. But something inside me shifted, like a room that had been emptied but still smelled like someone who used to live there.

For a long time, I thought healing would come from answers. From closure. From loud realizations and clean breaks. But it didn't. Healing came in the quiet. In the stillness. In the moments when no one was watching and I wasn't pretending anymore. It came when the noise faded and I finally had no choice but to sit with everything I had been running from.

At first, the silence was loud. It echoed. It brought your name back with every breath. But eventually, it softened. It stopped asking questions and started offering space. And in that space, I started to hear something new, my own voice.

I realized how long I had been waiting for someone else to see me before I saw myself. I had tied my worth to your presence, my peace to your approval, my meaning to your affection. But in the quiet, I began to untie those knots, gently, patiently, painfully.

I learned that love is beautiful, but it should never require you to disappear. That longing can be honest, but it doesn't always lead to something lasting. And that silence, though sharp at first, can teach you the most, not about them, but about you.

In the quiet, I met the parts of myself

I used to hide behind other people's laughter.

I learned to sit with my emptiness

without rushing to fill it.

I learned that missing someone

isn't a weakness,

but holding onto someone who let go is.

I stopped asking why they left,

and started asking why I stayed so long

in the spaces where I was shrinking.

In silence, I stopped waiting for permission to heal.

I just did.

The quiet showed me that peace doesn't come when the pain ends, it comes when you stop needing it to. It comes when you stop writing stories around people who've already closed their chapters. When you stop romanticizing what was never fully real, and start loving the version of yourself that survived it anyway.

There's a stillness that comes after heartbreak. A kind of quiet strength. You start to breathe differently. You walk a little slower, but with more awareness. You laugh, not louder, but truer. You begin to live for yourself, not in rebellion, but in recognition: I am still here. I made it through.

And maybe that's what the quiet was always trying to say. That nothing is missing from you. That the world keeps going not to forget them, but to remind you that you are more than what you lost. You always were.

Chapter 12:
I Loved You Gently

I didn't love you recklessly. I didn't rush in with fire or demand anything in return. I didn't throw my heart at your feet hoping you'd catch it. I simply... gave. Quietly. Gently. Without expectation. Without noise. Without the need for it to be anything more than what it was.

I loved you in the way I showed up. In the way I remembered the smallest things you said. In the way I listened, not just to your words, but to the silence between them. I loved you in stillness. Not to possess you, not to claim you, but to witness you. To see you fully and stay anyway.

You may never know the full weight of what that means. How rare it is to love without needing anything back. But I know. And that knowing, that kind of love, it left a mark on me.

There was nothing dramatic in the way I loved you. No scenes. No confessions under moonlight. Just presence. Just softness. Just truth. I loved you like a secret I was too careful with. And maybe that's why you never saw it clearly. Because I never made you uncomfortable with the depth of it. I loved you in a way that allowed you to breathe, and maybe that made it too easy to leave.

But I don't regret it.

Because gentle love isn't weak love. It takes strength to stay soft in a world that hardens you. It takes courage to love someone without knowing how, or if, they'll love you back. And if nothing else, I loved you honestly. That counts for something. Even if you didn't see it. Even if you never say it.

I loved you in the spaces between words,

in the pauses between "hello" and "goodbye."

I loved you without rushing,

without reason,

without a need to be loved in return.

I loved you in the quiet,

and when you left,

I grieved the silence we never filled.

But even now,

if someone asked me how I felt,

I wouldn't tell them I was broken.

I'd say,

I loved someone gently.

And that love lives quietly inside me still.

That's the thing about soft love, it doesn't beg to be remembered, but it lingers. It touches without leaving fingerprints. It doesn't fight for a place, but it leaves a presence.

I don't know if you'll ever think of me. If a scent or a song or a passing thought will remind you of what I was to you. But I hope, in some small way, you remember the gentleness. The way I cared. The way I stayed. The way I didn't ask you to be anything but yourself.

And maybe, just maybe, that's the purest kind of love there is, one that expects nothing, but offers everything anyway.

Chapter 13:
The Versions of You I Still Carry

You're not just one memory. You're many. You live in different versions of yourself, scattered across my past like bookmarks in a story I keep returning to, even when I know how it ends.

I carry the version of you that made me laugh at the smallest things. The one who listened without rushing, who made ordinary days feel like they were touched by something meaningful. I remember your voice when it was soft, curious, open. The way you said my name like it mattered. That version of you, the warm one, still feels like home I'm not allowed to visit anymore.

But I also carry the version of you that went quiet. The one who stopped looking me in the eyes. The one who started replying later and with fewer words. I remember that version too, not because I want to, but because I had to learn how to let go of someone who was already halfway gone.

There's a version of you I still miss. And there's a version I still try to forget.

That's the truth about love that doesn't last: it doesn't leave as one person, it leaves as pieces. You don't just mourn someone's absence; you mourn the life you imagined with them, the conversations that never happened, the better version of yourself you felt you were when they were near.

And yet… I don't hate any of those versions of you.

Because every version taught me something. The kind, early version reminded me of what it feels like to be seen. The fading version showed me what silence sounds like when someone stops choosing you. And all the versions in between taught me how deeply I could feel, even in confusion, even in loss.

You live in flashes now.

In the way my stomach still turns when I hear certain songs.

In the way some sunsets remind me of the way you once looked at the sky.

You're not here anymore, but you left footprints

in places you probably forgot you even stood.

And I still find you there.

Not fully. Not clearly.

Just pieces.

Just shadows.

Versions of you I never asked to keep,

but somehow still carry.

There's a version of you I'll always protect. The one I believed in. The one I loved, even in silence. And maybe it wasn't the full you, maybe it was the version I needed, or the one I created in moments of hope, but it mattered to me. And it shaped me.

Sometimes, I wonder if you do the same with me. If you remember me in fragments. If I live somewhere in your mind as laughter, or stillness, or the person who never asked you for anything but your presence. Maybe I do. Maybe I don't. I'll never know.

But I've made peace with the versions of you I still carry. I no longer ask them to stay. I no longer fight to forget. I just walk with them, quietly, like old friends who remind me where I've been, and why I had to keep going.

Chapter 14: The Art of Letting Go Without Closure

There are endings that feel like a conversation. Like something agreed upon, painful, maybe, but mutual. You talk. You cry. You part ways with some sense of understanding. And then... there are endings like this.

Endings that don't look like endings at all.

No final words. No apology. No clean break. Just distance. Just absence. Just someone slowly fading out of your life until all that's left is confusion and the echo of what they used to be.

That's the kind of ending I got with you.

For a long time, I waited. Not just for you to come back, but for you to explain. To say why. To give me even one sentence that made the silence make sense. I replayed every moment in my head, searching for clues, blaming myself, wondering if I misread everything. Was I too quiet? Too much? Not enough?

Closure became this thing I thought I needed to breathe again. Like if you could just say what changed, I'd stop aching. If you could just tell me how you stopped feeling what I still felt, I could stop feeling it too. But no explanation came. And so I was left to create one for myself, not because it would be true, but because the silence was eating me alive.

And that's when I learned the hardest truth of all: sometimes, you don't get closure. Sometimes, the apology never comes. The goodbye never happens. The questions never get answered. And you have to learn how to live with that.

You have to learn how to heal without the help of the person who hurt you. You have to learn how to stop checking your phone, stop waiting for the door to open, stop hoping that maybe, just maybe, they'll care enough to explain. Because if they were going to, they already would have.

And that is the closure.

Closure is not always a conversation.

Sometimes, it's the moment you stop begging the silence to speak.

It's the moment you accept

that some people leave without looking back,

and that has nothing to do with your worth.

Closure is not what they give you.

It's what you choose.

It's the decision to keep walking

even when your heart stays stuck in the past.

It's learning how to breathe

even when the air is full of things you never got to say.

I stopped asking why you disappeared. I stopped trying to decode the timing, or the shift in your voice, or the way your messages grew colder. I stopped blaming myself for your silence. And when I did, when I let go of the need for your version of the ending, something inside me slowly began to heal.

Letting go without closure doesn't mean you're okay. It doesn't mean the memories stop hurting. It just means you've decided to stop bleeding for someone who no longer holds the knife. It means you've chosen to carry the lesson instead of the weight.

The truth is, you can mourn someone who's still alive. You can miss someone who doesn't miss you. And you can still love someone while learning how to live without them.

I loved you. That part is real.

But so is this:

I let go.

Without answers.

Without clarity.

Without the kindness I gave being returned.

And still, I let go.

Because I deserve peace.

Because I deserve to be free from the story that never got its ending.

Because healing isn't about getting closure from them.

It's about giving closure to yourself.

Chapter 15: The Day I Stopped Waiting

It didn't happen all at once. It never does.

The day I stopped waiting for you wasn't marked by some dramatic realization, or a moment of sudden anger. It wasn't a midnight epiphany or a tearful breakdown. It was slower than that. Softer. Like forgetting a face you once knew by heart. Like waking up from a long dream and not remembering how it ended.

At first, it felt like betrayal, not of you, but of myself. Because waiting had become a ritual. A quiet part of my every day. I would check my phone with no real reason. Reread conversations we hadn't had in months. Revisit memories like they were still breathing. I held on, not because I didn't know better, but because I wasn't ready to let go of the hope. That maybe one day you'd remember me in a way that mattered. That maybe you'd realize what we were. What we could've been.

But time has a way of being louder than hope. And slowly, it started to whisper things I didn't want to hear, that you weren't coming back. That you'd already left, long before you stopped replying. That you were building a life in which I was no longer even a footnote.

And then one day, I didn't check my phone.

Not because I was trying not to, but because, for the first time in a long while, I forgot to. I got through an entire day without imagining you'd show up. Without replaying what I would say if you did. Without scanning every silence for your name.

It felt empty. And then it felt quiet. And then it felt… like peace.

I didn't know it then, but that was the day I stopped waiting.

It wasn't an announcement. I didn't tell anyone. I didn't write it down. It was a decision made deep in my bones, in the place where hope used to sit, now filled with something stronger: acceptance.

I didn't stop loving you that day. But I stopped loving the idea that you would come back.

I stopped waiting for the text, the apology, the explanation. I stopped checking if you watched my stories. I stopped hoping that a version of you, the one I believed in, would appear and undo everything that had already been done.

You didn't choose me.

Not fully.

Not when it mattered.

And that truth, as painful as it was,

was the beginning of my freedom.

Because I finally saw

that love isn't waiting in the dark

for someone to remember you.

It's walking into the light

even if you're walking alone.

The day I stopped waiting, I started coming back to myself.

I took a longer breath. I stepped into conversations without wondering if your name would appear in them. I laughed, not to forget you, but because something in me felt light again. I didn't have to rehearse the past anymore. I didn't have to explain you to myself.

You were gone. And I was still here.

That truth used to ache. Now it makes me proud.

I waited because I loved you. But I stopped waiting because I finally loved myself more. I realized that I didn't need someone to return to me in order to be whole. I didn't need a second chance to make the first one count. I gave what I could. I stayed as long as I should. And when it was time, I left, quietly, gently, fully.

Healing didn't look like forgetting.

It looked like choosing myself

without waiting for permission.

It looked like standing at the door

I once hoped you'd walk through,

and finally,

closing it.

Chapter 16:
The Way I Love Now

The way I love now... is different.

Not colder. Not harder. Just quieter. Wiser. Slower. I've learned that love isn't about the rush, it's about the rhythm. And that sometimes, the most powerful kind of love doesn't arrive in fireworks or chaos, but in steadiness. In someone who stays. In someone who sees you without needing to fix you. In someone who knows that love is not possession, it is presence.

I didn't used to know that. I used to give love like it was proof. Like if I just loved someone enough, I could convince them not to leave. I used to give too much, too fast. I used to mistake attention for affection, and silence for patience. I gave and gave, even when my hands were empty. I waited for someone to meet me where I already was, instead of learning to love in a way that protected me too.

But now?

Now I know what love should feel like, and what it shouldn't cost.

I've learned that real love doesn't require you to shrink. It doesn't ask you to prove your worth through sacrifice. It doesn't wait until you're hurting to show up. And most importantly, it doesn't leave you guessing. Love isn't a riddle. It's a presence. If it's real, you won't need to wonder.

The way I love now has boundaries. Not walls, just doors with locks that I choose when to open. I still believe in vulnerability. I still believe in softness. But I no longer confuse being available with being enough. I've stopped showing up for people who won't stay. I've stopped explaining my value to those who can't see it. And I've stopped waiting to be chosen, because now I choose myself, every time.

There was a time I would've given everything to hear from you again. A time when your name could unravel me in an instant. A time when I still believed that if you came back, things could be whole again. But I don't live in that time anymore.

Now, when I think of you, it's with gratitude and distance. You taught me how deeply I could feel, and how deeply I could break. You taught me how silence can be both safety and suffocation. You showed me what happens when love is real in one heart but not returned in another. And that lesson, though it broke me, rebuilt me too.

I don't need grand promises anymore. I need consistency. I need someone whose love doesn't depend on perfect timing or flawless days. I need quiet understanding. Laughter that feels like healing. Someone who speaks when things are hard, not just when they're easy. I want a love that grows in the sunlight and survives the storms, not one that disappears at the first sign of rain.

The way I love now

is with patience,

with presence,

with peace.

Not to win someone over,

but to honor what I hold inside me.

Not to prove my worth,

but because I know it.

I don't need saving.

I just need someone who chooses to stay.

Not because they have to,

but because they want to.

I've learned that love is not the solution to emptiness. It is not meant to fix your wounds or silence your fears. Love is not the answer to pain. It is the companion you meet after you've made peace with the silence. After you've looked yourself in the eye and said, I am enough, even alone.

That's where I love from now, not from lack, but from wholeness. Not from desperation, but from devotion. I want love to be a partnership, not a rescue. I want us to be two people who have healed enough to build something beautiful, not two broken halves clinging to each other for air.

I still believe in love.

But the way I love now is rooted, not reckless. It is clear, not chaotic. It is honest, even when it trembles. It is not afraid to speak, not afraid to leave if unvalued, and not afraid to stay when it's real.

I've changed.

And so has the way I love.

But what hasn't changed is this:

I still love fully.

Still deeply.

Still with everything I have.

But now,

I love without losing myself in the process.

Chapter 17: How I Forgave You (Even Without an Apology)

Forgiveness isn't always the final step in healing. Sometimes, it's the first. Sometimes, it's the only thing that lets you begin.

For a long time, I didn't think I needed to forgive you. I thought what I needed was an explanation. Something that made sense. A reason, a why, a sentence that could put all the broken pieces into a single paragraph. But none of that ever came.

You left in fragments, not just from my life, but from the version of myself that trusted too easily. You vanished quietly, without apology, without warning. And in the vacuum you left, I filled the silence with my own blame.

Maybe it was me. Maybe I should've said more. Maybe I should've been less quiet, or more obvious. Maybe I asked for too little. Or too much. Or maybe I was never really seen at all, just convenient, just comfortable, just there.

That kind of thinking stays with you. It crawls under your skin. It makes you question your worth, your memory, your ability to love. And for a while, I let it. I gave your absence permission to define me. I made your silence my reflection.

But silence doesn't carry truth. It only carries shadows.

And slowly, I began to understand, the apology I needed wasn't coming. Not because I didn't deserve it, but because some people never offer what they should. Some people walk away with the peace they stole from you and never look back.

And still, I forgave you.

Not loudly. Not overnight. But piece by piece, I loosened the weight of what I was never given.

Because forgiveness, I realized, isn't about them. It's about setting down the story you've been carrying for too long. It's about choosing not to be bitter in a world that gives you every reason to be. It's about reclaiming your voice, your peace, your life, and doing it without needing permission.

I forgave you

when I stopped rehearsing arguments

you never showed up to hear.

I forgave you

when I stopped checking the door

hoping you'd return with answers.

I forgave you

when I realized my pain didn't need your apology

to be real,

it just needed my acceptance

to stop bleeding.

There is something powerful about forgiving someone in silence. When they don't even know you've done it. When they're out there living a life you're no longer part of, and you're finally okay with that. Not because it didn't matter, but because you matter more.

I didn't forgive you to let you back in. I forgave you to walk away without dragging your shadow behind me. I forgave you to sleep again without wondering what I did wrong. I forgave you so my future wouldn't have to carry your ghost.

And if I'm being honest, forgiveness didn't mean forgetting. I still remember. I still feel. But I no longer hurt. And that's the difference.

I've made peace with the fact that I'll never get the words I once begged for. And maybe that's what healing really looks like, choosing peace over answers. Choosing to close the chapter without needing to rewrite the ending.

Because not every story deserves closure. Some stories deserve freedom.

I forgive you,

not because you earned it,

but because I won't spend another season

waiting for you to realize what you lost.

I forgive you,

not because it was okay,

but because I am okay now.

I forgive you,

because I'm tired of dragging your silence

through the parts of my life

that finally feel like mine again.

It took time. More than I care to admit. But one day, I woke up and realized I hadn't thought of you in a while. And when I did, it didn't sting. It didn't ache. It just… passed through me, like a song I used to know by heart.

You became a chapter in my story, not the ending, not even the main plot. Just a moment. One I grew from. One I survived.

I hope, wherever you are, you found what you were looking for. But even if you didn't, that's no longer my burden to carry.

I'm free now.

And that freedom is mine, not because of you, but in spite of you.

Chapter 18: The Kind of Love I Deserve

There's a moment, somewhere between heartbreak and healing, when you stop asking why they left and start asking what you deserve. It's a quiet shift, one that sneaks in after the ache begins to fade. And suddenly, you're not thinking about them anymore, you're thinking about yourself. Not the version of you that waited, or pleaded, or tried to hold together something that was already falling apart, but the version that's still standing. The one who survived.

That's the version I became. And that's the version who started asking harder questions.

Not about them. But about me.

Why did I give so much of myself without being met halfway? Why did I tolerate uncertainty, inconsistency, silence? Why did I call that love, when it was barely even care?

And maybe the answer is simple: I hadn't yet learned what I deserved. I only knew what I hoped for. I had loved from a place of fear, fear of losing, fear of being alone, fear that love doesn't come around often so I should hold onto whatever form it takes.

But I know better now.

I've seen what it feels like to give love to someone who doesn't know how to hold it. I've watched myself disappear just to make space for someone else's comfort. I've silenced my own needs, postponed my own healing, twisted myself into versions I no longer recognize, just to keep someone close who was already drifting.

And I won't do that again.

Because the kind of love I deserve doesn't make me doubt myself. It doesn't require me to guess where I stand. It doesn't punish me for being vulnerable, or make me afraid of asking for the simplest things, honesty, effort, presence.

The kind of love I deserve is not perfect. It doesn't always have the right words. But it shows up. It stays. It communicates, even when things are hard. It makes space for my feelings, and trusts me enough to bring its own. It chooses growth over pride, listening over silence, and clarity over confusion.

I deserve a love that makes me feel safe, not just physically, but emotionally. A love where I don't have to carry both hearts. Where I don't have to apologize for needing reassurance. Where I don't feel like I'm walking on eggshells just to avoid being too much.

I deserve a love that celebrates who I am, not one that tolerates me until I change. A love that respects my mind, understands my past, and still leans in. One that doesn't flinch at my scars, but asks how I got them, and stays through the telling.

I deserve a love that grows with me, not one that holds me hostage to who I used to be. One that walks beside me, not ahead or behind. One that doesn't compete, but supports. That doesn't run when things get quiet or complicated. A love that knows how to stay, not just arrive.

And I'm no longer afraid to say that out loud.

Because for so long, I thought asking for the love I wanted made me difficult. Needy. Demanding. But now I see it differently. I see that clarity is not a burden, it's a boundary. I'm not asking for a fairytale. I'm asking for something real. Something stable. Something mutual.

That's not too much.

That's the bare minimum.

And maybe I had to lose myself to learn that. Maybe I had to break in all the places I tried to hold someone else together. Maybe

I had to be left without answers, without closure, without apologies, just so I could learn how to never leave myself again.

Because now I know what I bring. I know what I offer. I know the depth, the loyalty, the tenderness I give, and I will no longer pour that into someone who can't return it.

The kind of love I deserve is not about fireworks or fairytales.

It's about respect. Consistency. Partnership. It's about choosing each other, over and over, especially when things are hard.

And I won't settle for anything less than that again.

Chapter 19: If You Ever Think of Me Again

If you ever think of me again, I hope it's in quiet moments. Not in chaos. Not in guilt. Just quiet, the way I loved you. The way I stayed. The way I never asked for more than what you were willing to give, even when it broke me.

I wonder if you ever do. Not every day. Not even often. Just… sometimes. When a certain song plays. When you hear a joke only I would've laughed at. When the light hits the room the way it used to when we were still something unspoken, unfinished, unnamed.

I wonder if you remember the version of me who waited, who believed that maybe you just needed time, or space, or healing. The version of me who never stopped showing up, even when it became clear that you were slowly learning how to live without me. Maybe you don't remember it like that. Maybe it doesn't stand out to you at all. That's okay. I've stopped needing your memory to validate my truth.

Still, sometimes I wonder what it would feel like if, one random afternoon, you paused mid-conversation with someone new and thought, "They used to know me that way." If, just for a moment, you missed the way I understood you, even in your silence. Even in the distance. Even when you didn't ask me to.

If you ever think of me again, I don't want it to be out of regret. I don't need your sorrow. I'm not looking for apologies that come too late or confessions that can't undo the damage. I've made peace with the fact that we existed the way we did, unfinished and fragile and real, even if not lasting. What we were mattered, even if you never said it.

And if you ever look back, I hope you realize I never tried to change you. I didn't fall in love with a future version of you or an idea of who you might become. I loved you as you were. In the mess, in the confusion, in the stillness. I didn't need perfection. I just needed presence. But in the end, even that was too much to ask.

I don't think you were cruel. Just careless. Careless with my heart, with my hope, with the time I spent trying to fill in the blanks your silence left behind. Maybe you didn't know what to do with the kind of love I offered. Or maybe you thought it would always be there, waiting, patient, unshaken. But nothing, not even quiet love, waits forever.

If you ever think of me again, I hope it's with kindness. I hope you remember the way I loved, not loudly, but fully. The way I never asked you to be anything but yourself. The way I noticed the things you never said and still stayed anyway. I hope you remember the softness, even if you never knew what to do with it.

I've changed since then. I've grown. I no longer wait for someone to remember me in order to feel remembered. I no longer break myself open for people who don't know how to hold what I give. I've stopped needing to be seen in places where I was only ever looked at.

But I still carry a small part of you, not with longing, not with pain, just… awareness. A gentle truth that we shared something, however brief, that shaped the way I now love. The way I now walk into rooms. The way I now leave, when I am no longer met with the same care I offer.

So if you ever think of me again, know this: I'm no longer hurting. I'm not angry. I'm not waiting. I'm just living, fully, deeply, honestly. And I hope you are too.

I hope, in your own way, you found what you were looking for.

And if one day you find yourself wondering about me, about us, I hope you remember that someone, once, loved you without needing anything in return. Someone once saw the parts of you that even you avoided. And that someone walked away, not because they stopped loving you, but because they finally started loving themselves.

If you ever think of me again…

I hope it makes you quiet.

Not sad. Just still.

Still enough to remember what real love once looked like, even if you didn't recognize it at the time.

Chapter 20: The Things I Never Said Aloud

There are things I never said. Words that lived in the back of my throat, quiet and unfinished, because I was always afraid they'd push you further away. Because I convinced myself that silence would keep you closer, even though, in the end, it didn't.

I didn't tell you how much it hurt when you pulled away. How I noticed, long before it was obvious. How I felt the shift in the way you spoke to me, the pauses, the delayed replies, the way your eyes stopped holding mine for longer than a second. I never said anything because I was scared that acknowledging the distance would make it real. So I smiled through it. I stayed soft. I stayed near. I let the silence stretch between us until it swallowed everything.

I didn't tell you that I needed more. Not more things, not more promises, just more of you. More presence. More honesty. More intention. I didn't say it out loud because I thought it would make me sound needy. Because I thought maybe love wasn't supposed to ask for anything at all. But the truth is, I was starving, and calling it patience.

I didn't tell you how much I missed the version of you that made me feel safe. The version that saw me. That laughed with me. That asked questions and actually waited for the answer. I didn't know how to say that you were still there, but somehow already gone. I didn't know how to explain the heartbreak of losing someone who was still sitting right in front of me.

I didn't tell you that I was afraid. Afraid of losing you. Afraid of being forgotten. Afraid that I had imagined the entire thing, that the connection, the closeness, the depth, had only lived in my mind. I stayed quiet because I didn't want to seem insecure. But inside, I was unraveling.

I didn't tell you how angry I was. Not just at you, but at myself. For ignoring the red flags. For giving too many chances. For romanticizing the good days just to survive the bad ones. I carried that anger in silence, and it turned into sadness. The kind of sadness that doesn't scream, but lingers in the quiet hours of the night when your name still shows up uninvited.

I never told you how much I hoped. How every little thing you did, a message, a glance, a soft laugh, became something I held onto like a lifeline. I gave meaning to crumbs. I built stories out of moments that probably meant nothing to you. But to me, they were everything. They were proof that maybe, just maybe, you still felt something too.

I never asked you why. Why you drifted. Why you changed. Why you didn't say goodbye. I told myself I didn't need to know, that closure wasn't something I had to beg for. But the truth is, I had a thousand questions, and the silence they sat in became heavier than the answers would have ever been.

I didn't tell you that I loved you. Not in those words. I thought showing up for you was enough. I thought being consistent, kind, and understanding would somehow say it for me. But now I wonder, would it have changed anything if I had said it aloud? Or would it have only hurt more when you walked away anyway?

I didn't tell you how proud I was of the parts of you you never saw in yourself. I didn't tell you how your presence made the ordinary feel sacred. I didn't tell you that some of the best parts of my day were the ones you didn't even realize you touched. I didn't say those things, because I was afraid they would make you uncomfortable. And maybe they would have. But maybe they also would've reminded you what it felt like to be seen.

There's a strange kind of grief that comes from holding too much inside. From silencing your own heart in the hope that someone else will speak first. And that's what I lived with for so long, a mouth full of unspoken truth, a heart weighed down by unsent letters, unanswered questions, unread moments.

But now, I'm saying it all, not for you, but for me.

Because I deserve to let it out. I deserve to name what I carried. To own my voice again. To stop pretending that staying quiet was strength, when it was really just fear dressed up as grace.

The things I never said aloud don't hurt the same way anymore. Now they're not ghosts, they're reminders. Reminders of the version of me that loved without limits, even when it was hard. Even when it wasn't returned. Even when it meant carrying the weight alone.

And that version of me, the one who felt deeply and stayed soft through it all, deserves to be heard. Even now. Even here.

Even if it's just in a chapter no one else will ever read.

Chapter 21: The Silence I Needed to Hear

For most of my life, silence felt like punishment. A signal that something had gone wrong. That someone had turned away. That I wasn't enough, or too much, or somehow both. I used to fill silence with assumptions, with imagined conversations, fears, regrets, desperate hope. When someone went quiet, I would spiral into their silence, trying to read between the lines of what was never said.

That's the kind of silence I knew with you, the kind that left me pacing my thoughts at night, replaying every word we'd ever spoken, trying to find the moment where it started to fall apart. The kind that made my chest tighten, because I couldn't tell if your silence was temporary or forever. And when it turned out to be forever, I had to learn how to breathe in the emptiness you left behind.

But something strange happened after you were gone.

The silence stayed. And for a while, I hated it. It felt too loud. Too heavy. But with time, something shifted. That same silence I once feared slowly started to feel different, less like a threat, more like space. Less like punishment, more like permission. I began to realize I wasn't drowning in your absence anymore. I was finally learning how to sit with my own presence.

Silence no longer meant "I'm waiting."

It meant "I'm listening."

Not to you.

To me.

For the first time in a long time, I could hear myself think, and more importantly, feel. I wasn't filtering my emotions through someone else's comfort. I wasn't softening my sadness to make someone stay. I wasn't choosing silence as a way to be loved. I was simply… silent. On my own. And somehow, not lonely.

That's when I knew the healing had begun, not when I stopped thinking of you, but when I could sit in the stillness you left behind and not ache for it to be filled.

Because healing doesn't always look like movement. Sometimes, it looks like stillness. Like sitting in the same place where you once fell apart and realizing, this time, you don't need anyone to come and rescue you.

This is the silence I needed to hear: the silence that reminded me of my own voice.

The silence that let me cry without explaining.

That let me laugh without guilt.

That let me grieve what was, without begging for what could've been.

I used to think I needed answers.

That if I could just hear your voice one more time, I'd finally understand.

But now I know: understanding doesn't always come from words.

Sometimes, it comes from the quiet.

From the way you finally stop asking why and start asking, "What now?"

The silence taught me how to stop reaching for what isn't reaching back.

How to close chapters without closure.

How to be enough, even when no one is watching.

This silence, the one I feared, the one I ran from, became the place where I found myself again.

I no longer need noise to feel alive.

I no longer need attention to feel seen.

And I no longer need someone else to speak my worth into existence.

The silence did that.

The silence gave me back my name.

Chapter 22: What I Know About Love Now

Love used to be a mystery to me, a blur of emotions, a storm I threw myself into without checking the weather. I once believed that love was supposed to be chaotic, overwhelming, all-consuming. I thought love had to hurt a little to feel real. I confused intensity with intimacy. I mistook longing for loyalty. I believed that the more I gave, the more someone would stay.

But now, I know better. Because now, I know love.

Not the idea of it. Not the fantasy. Not the version I once begged from someone who couldn't give it. But the truth of it, calm, quiet, real.

I know that love isn't about proving yourself. You don't need to chase it, shrink for it, wait endlessly in silence for it to arrive. Real love doesn't ask you to erase yourself just to fit into someone else's life. It doesn't reward you for sacrificing your needs. It doesn't measure your worth by how long you can stay silent while hurting.

Love shows up. It doesn't leave you wondering. It doesn't speak in mixed signals and then blame you for misunderstanding. It doesn't make you feel like you're always one misstep away from being too much. When it's real, love feels like clarity, not confusion.

I used to think love had to be earned. That if I was just more patient, more kind, more forgiving, someone would finally stay. I used to believe that if I loved someone enough, it would heal them, or make them choose me. But that's not how love works. Love is not manipulation. It is not sacrifice without balance. It's not giving until you're empty.

What I know about love now is this: it meets you where you are. It sees your wounds and doesn't flinch. It listens without trying to fix or flee. It doesn't play games with your heart. It doesn't leave when things get uncomfortable. Love, when it's real, leans in, not out.

I know now that love is freedom, not control. It's not about owning someone or being owned. It's about choosing each other, freely, again and again. It's about saying, "I'm here," not because you have to be, but because you want to be. And meaning it.

Love isn't perfect. It doesn't always come with the right words, and sometimes it takes time to learn each other's language.

But even in its imperfection, real love is consistent. You don't have to beg it to stay. You don't have to lose your voice to keep it.

The love I want now, the love I know I deserve, is the kind that builds, not breaks. The kind that softens, not shatters. The kind that holds space for who I am now, not who someone wishes I would be. It's a love that sees my strength, but doesn't expect me to always be strong. It's a love that celebrates softness, that doesn't fear depth, that knows the beauty of showing up even on the hard days.

I've learned that love doesn't come to fix your life. It comes to walk beside you in it. You still have to do your own healing. You still have to know who you are without it. But when it's real, love makes the journey a little lighter. A little warmer. A little more worth it.

And I've learned this too: the first love you ever need to get right is the one you have with yourself.

Because if you don't know how to treat yourself with kindness, you'll accept love that mirrors your own self-doubt. If you don't believe in your worth, you'll hand your heart to people who don't value it either. But when you learn how to love yourself, truly, deeply, without condition, you stop settling. You stop begging. You stop chasing ghosts.

And you wait for the love that feels like home, not the one that burns you and calls it passion.

What I know about love now is this:

It's not loud.

It's not rushed.

It's not built on fear or urgency.

It's steady.

It's present.

It's soft, but never weak.

It holds you in your joy and your mess.

It doesn't make you feel small to feel wanted.

It reminds you that you are already whole.

Chapter 23: I Don't Miss You Anymore

I used to miss you in the smallest moments. In the sound of your laugh echoing in my memory, in the space beside me where you never really sat but always belonged. I used to miss you in ways that hurt quietly, like a soft ache under the skin, like breathing with a weight in my chest I couldn't explain to anyone else.

There were days I'd wake up and you'd be the first thought. Not because I wanted you back, but because some part of me was still tangled in the way things ended, or didn't end, between us. I'd carry your name silently through my routines, trying not to let it spill out in conversations, even when everything reminded me of you.

I missed you in songs. In half-written sentences. In memories I didn't ask to revisit. I missed you when I saw someone smile the way you used to. When I read something I knew you would've loved. When life handed me something beautiful and my first instinct was to tell you, before I remembered there was no "you" to tell anymore.

I missed the version of you that made me feel like I wasn't hard to love. The version that leaned in instead of pulling away. The version that stayed soft when everything else in the world felt rough. And maybe what I really missed wasn't even you, maybe it was the version of me that believed we were something real.

But that version of me doesn't live here anymore.

I don't miss you now. And I don't say that with anger. I say it with peace. The kind of peace that comes after a long storm. The kind that you only earn by sitting with every unanswered question, every quiet rejection, every silent goodbye.

I don't miss you because I no longer need you to understand what I went through. I no longer carry your name like an open wound. I no longer replay our conversations hoping they'll sound different the hundredth time around.

You became a part of my story, not the whole thing.

There was a time when missing you was part of my identity. When letting go felt like betrayal. But healing is strange. It doesn't announce itself. It just… shows up one day, in the way you no longer flinch at their name. In the way your chest feels light where it used to be tight. In the way you can talk about the past without tasting bitterness.

I don't miss you because I no longer wish you were here. I don't want the past back. I don't need the apology that never came. I've stopped building futures on broken foundations. I've stopped writing letters you'll never read.

And I've stopped hoping you'd change your mind.

I don't miss you because I've built a life that no longer has space for people who leave without looking back. I've filled the silence you left with my own voice. I've filled the emptiness with presence, with peace, with people who choose me without hesitation.

What I had with you taught me a lot. About love. About loss. About how far I'm willing to go for someone, and how far I should never go again.

You were a lesson. A beautiful, painful, necessary one. But that chapter has closed.

And no, I don't miss you.

Not anymore.

Because now, I finally remember what it feels like

to belong to myself again.

Chapter 24:
If We Had Met at a Different Time

Sometimes I wonder what we could have been if life had introduced us differently, if we had met later, or earlier, or in a moment that didn't demand so much from us before we even had the chance to begin.

If we had met at a different time, would we have understood each other better? Would we have had the language to speak what we felt, instead of hoping the other person would just know? Would we have had the emotional vocabulary to say, "I'm not okay," instead of withdrawing into silence? Would we have stayed, if staying didn't feel so heavy?

There are versions of us I still imagine, not because I want to go back, but because part of healing is learning to accept that love isn't always lost because it wasn't real. Sometimes it's lost because we weren't ready. Because life hadn't taught us what we needed to know yet. Because we didn't yet understand how to love someone without disappearing inside them.

If we had met at a different time, maybe we would've been less guarded. Less tired. Less bruised by the ones who came before. Maybe we wouldn't have been so afraid to ask for what we needed. Maybe we would've believed we were worthy of being chosen, not just once, but every day, without question.

In another life, maybe we would've met when the world felt less loud. When our hearts weren't still learning how to unlearn the damage. When we weren't so determined to protect ourselves from the very thing we craved most.

Maybe then I wouldn't have flinched when you got close. Maybe you wouldn't have shut down when things got real. Maybe we would've sat in the hard conversations instead of running from them. Maybe I would've let you in sooner. Maybe you wouldn't have left so quietly.

But we didn't meet at that time. We met in the middle of our chaos. We crossed paths when we were still carrying too many pieces of other people. When we were still trying to figure out who we were alone, let alone together. We met at a time when neither of us had enough to offer, but both of us wanted so badly to be understood.

And maybe that's why it felt so intense. So familiar. Because we recognized the hunger in each other. The ache. The tiredness.

The hope. But recognition is not always readiness. You can see someone's soul and still not know how to hold it.

If we had met at a different time, maybe I would've been more patient. Maybe you would've been more honest. Maybe we wouldn't have let silence grow between us like a wall. Maybe we would've learned how to stay instead of how to leave quietly.

But here's what I've come to understand: timing doesn't change truth. Even if we had met later, or sooner, we would still be who we were then. And sometimes, love doesn't survive who we are before we've grown.

Still, it's strange, how some people leave, but never really go. How even now, after all the healing, your name still lives in the quiet corners of what-ifs. I don't wish for you anymore, but I still wonder. And I think that's okay.

I've stopped needing closure from you. I've stopped needing answers to the questions I used to lose sleep over. But sometimes, late at night, I still wonder what we could've been if the world had been softer, if we had been older, calmer, braver. If we had met after learning the lessons we learned too late.

Maybe in a different time, we wouldn't have hurt each other trying to hold on. Maybe we wouldn't have had to unlove each other just to survive.

Or maybe, in a different time… we never would've met at all.

And somehow, even that feels okay too.

Because whatever it was, it mattered. Even if it didn't last. Even if it couldn't. Even if it was only meant to be a chapter, not the ending.

Chapter 25: I Still Carry You in Small Ways

There are days I go without thinking of you at all. I move through them fully present, fully here, no shadow of your voice lingering in the corners of my mind. I laugh. I work. I breathe deeply. And I don't look for you in any of it.

But then, suddenly, without warning, you return.

Not in some grand, overwhelming wave. Not in sorrow or longing. Just... gently. In the way I turn toward the window when it rains. In the way I pause before responding when someone says something with too much meaning. In the moment between inhale and exhale, where something in me still remembers how it used to feel to carry you in my breath.

I no longer ache for you. I no longer miss you in the way I once did, not in the way that kept me up at night, trying to rewrite endings that had already been written. But I've come to accept something softer, something quieter: I still carry you, just not in the way I used to.

You live now in my patience, in the way I listen a little longer to the people I love. Because I know what it feels like to speak into silence. You live in the way I no longer chase people who don't make space for me. Because I know what it costs to keep showing up where I'm not truly seen.

You're in the way I protect my heart, not out of fear, but out of wisdom. Because I learned, with you, what happens when I give too much too quickly. When I pour from a cup that no one thinks to refill. I don't resent you for that. I just see it now, and I carry the lesson with care.

You live in the way I love now, slower, deeper, more deliberately. Because I once loved someone without guardrails, without pause, without asking if they could hold what I was giving. And I learned. I learned the difference between vulnerability and self-sacrifice. Between staying soft and staying silent.

You live in the way I leave now, not in anger, but in peace. When someone can't meet me where I stand, I don't beg them to rise anymore. I let them go. Because I know what it feels like to hold on too tightly to someone who was already halfway out the door. I've done that. I won't do it again.

Sometimes I hear a song that reminds me of you. Sometimes I walk by a place and remember a conversation, a glance, a laugh I didn't know would be one of the last. I don't turn away from those memories. I don't drown in them either. I just acknowledge them, like old photographs in a drawer I no longer need to open, but no longer fear.

You live in the spaces of me you unknowingly shaped. The lines I don't cross now. The questions I ask sooner. The silence I don't settle for. I carry you in the warnings I whisper to myself when I feel myself slipping into old patterns. And I carry you in the grace I give to others who are still learning how to love.

You're not a wound anymore. You're a thread, a small, quiet thread woven into the fabric of who I am. And I've come to realize that some people don't leave clean. They leave in echoes. In instincts. In habits. In the ways we now move differently through the world.

I don't wish for you to return. I don't need a conversation or a closure. I've made peace with the fact that what we had was real, and that it ended. Both can be true. And both have shaped me.

If someone were to ask me if I still think about you, I don't think I'd say yes. But I wouldn't say no either.

Because you're still here, not in my heart, but in my hands. In the way I hold others now. In the way I hold myself.

I don't carry the weight of what we were.

I carry the quiet lessons of what we became.

And I think, in some strange and human way, that's a kind of love, too.

Chapter 26: I Needed to Lose You to Find Myself

There was a time I thought losing you would break me. And for a while, it did. It broke my routines. It broke my trust. It broke the soft, unquestioning way I used to love, without walls, without doubt, without wondering if I was enough.

In the beginning, the pain felt like drowning. It came in waves I couldn't predict. Some days I missed you so fiercely, I'd forget who I was without you. Other days, I'd pretend none of it mattered, only to collapse into silence the second I was alone. Healing wasn't linear. It wasn't poetic. It was messy and slow and exhausting.

But somewhere in that process, somewhere between losing you and learning how to breathe without you, something remarkable happened.

I met myself.

Not the version I was when I loved you. Not the one who waited for replies or softened her truth just to keep peace. Not the one who hoped you'd notice what she never dared to say aloud.

I met the version of me who didn't need to be chosen to feel worthy.

The one who began to ask, "What do I want?" instead of "What if they leave?"

The one who stopped tying her identity to being needed.

The one who learned that silence doesn't mean failure, it can also mean freedom.

And the deeper I went into that loneliness, the more I uncovered. Pieces of myself I had set aside to make room for you. Desires I had buried under compromise. Dreams I had paused because your love felt more urgent than my own voice. I didn't realize how far I'd drifted from myself, until you left.

But the truth is: I was never really whole while loving you. I was just good at pretending I didn't notice the emptiness. I made your presence a reason to avoid facing my own reflection. I wrapped myself around you, thinking if I gave enough, you'd stay. But love, when it's real, doesn't ask you to disappear.

And losing you forced me to reappear.

I learned how to sit in stillness without begging it to end. I learned how to hold my own heart without waiting for someone else to do it. I learned that peace isn't found in someone else's promise, it's found in the way you promise yourself not to settle anymore.

I used to think losing you was the tragedy. But now I see, it was the invitation.

To come home to myself.

To see the truth I had been hiding from.

To stop chasing love that cost me my own reflection.

There are still days when something reminds me of what we had. But now, instead of pain, I feel clarity. Not because you gave me closure, but because I finally gave it to myself.

I know now: the love I was searching for in you, I needed to find within.

And I did.

I found it in the quiet mornings where I didn't wake up hoping someone had texted.

In the way I began to speak more kindly to myself.

In the friendships that felt like calm instead of comparison.

In the joy that returned, slow, but certain, when I stopped trying to prove my worth.

I found it in the way I now walk away from what doesn't feel mutual.

In the way I no longer tolerate being half-held.

In the way I've made peace with the parts of me that once felt too much.

So no, losing you didn't ruin me.

It revealed me.

And for that, I will always be grateful.

Chapter 27: Some Goodbyes Aren't Loud

Not all goodbyes come crashing down like storms. Some don't arrive with closure, or explanations, or final words wrapped in clarity. Some goodbyes happen in silence, in pauses that stretch too long, in habits that fade, in glances that stop lingering.

Some goodbyes are so quiet, you don't even realize they're happening until the person is already gone.

That's how it was with you.

There was no dramatic ending. No big confrontation. No last argument. Just a slow, subtle unraveling. A steady quieting of everything we used to be. I didn't even notice it at first. I kept showing up to the conversation, to the moments, to the connection not realizing I was the only one still doing so.

You stopped replying the way you used to. You started laughing at different jokes. Your eyes didn't search for mine anymore. The energy shifted not all at once, but gradually. Like someone turning down the volume on a song you used to love, until one day, it's just… not playing anymore.

That kind of goodbye is hard to name.

Hard to mourn.

Because there's nothing to point to.

No breaking point.

No moment when it all shattered.

Just a quiet drifting.

Just distance disguised as routine.

And so, for a long time, I stayed.

Not because it still felt right,

but because it didn't feel wrong enough to leave.

That's the danger of subtle goodbyes, they trick you into thinking you're still holding something whole, even as it crumbles in your hands.

There's no goodbye to mark on a calendar. No anniversary of when it ended. Just memories that stop feeling warm. Conversations that stop feeling safe. A kind of loneliness that grows even in the presence of the person you once loved.

Eventually, I had to name it. Not for you. For me.

I had to admit to myself that it was over, not in a moment, but in the absence of one.

And that hurt in its own unique way. Because when someone walks away without saying goodbye, the grief has nowhere to go. It sits inside you. It lingers. You carry it like an unfinished sentence.

I wanted to be angry. I wanted to demand answers. But the truth is, I didn't need either. I just needed to accept what had already happened even if it didn't look like the goodbyes I was used to.

Because here's what I've learned:

Some people don't slam doors when they leave.

Some people just stop showing up.

And you won't always get a reason.

You won't always get the dignity of closure.

But you still have to choose your peace.

I stopped waiting for a conversation that was never coming.

I stopped trying to reopen a door that had slowly, gently closed.

And I stopped pretending that silence didn't mean something.

Some goodbyes are not loud.

But they still echo.

They still leave empty chairs at tables.

They still leave a question mark where a period should have been.

And sometimes, you don't get to say goodbye back.

Sometimes, your only response is how you move on.

How you heal.

How you refuse to chase someone who taught you through their absence that you were already enough.

That was the goodbye.

It wasn't a moment.

It was a realization.

And it was quiet.

But I heard it, finally.

And I answered back, not with words, but with release.

Chapter 28: Some Things Don't Deserve a Second Chance

We're taught to believe in second chances. That if something is meant for us, it will return. That timing can change everything. That love deserves more than one try. And for a long time, I believed that. I held onto that hope the way some people hold their breath underwater long enough to drown, waiting for the surface.

But there comes a moment when you realize... not everything that leaves should come back.

Some things, some people, some chapters, some versions of yourself don't deserve a second chance. Not because they were entirely bad. Not because the memories don't still pull at you sometimes. But because going back would cost you more than it ever gave you.

I used to replay it all in my head, the way we laughed, the softness in your voice on certain days, the warmth of your presence before things changed. I'd convince myself that maybe if we had just been different, maybe if the timing had been better, maybe if we had loved more gently... maybe it could've worked.

But the truth is, it didn't.

And it didn't for a reason.

You taught me how deeply I could feel. But you also taught me what it feels like to question my worth. You taught me what it's like to stay silent out of fear. To love carefully, cautiously afraid that one wrong word might make you leave. That's not love. That's survival dressed in affection.

I let so much slide just to keep the connection alive. I ignored red flags and called them challenges. I mistook inconsistency for mystery. I confused your absence for emotional depth as if your distance made you complex, not just unwilling.

But love isn't supposed to confuse you. It's not meant to keep you guessing. Real love doesn't leave you exhausted. It doesn't make you earn its presence.

So no, some things don't deserve a second chance.

Not because they never mattered.

But because they mattered enough to teach you what you never want again.

If you had come back, if you had said all the right things, I don't know what I would've done a year ago. Maybe I would've said yes. Maybe I would've given us another try, told myself people change. Maybe I would've started all over ignoring everything I had learned, just for the comfort of something familiar.

But not now.

Because now, I know what peace feels like.

Now, I know what it's like to not wake up wondering if I'm too much.

Now, I know how to hold myself fully without shrinking to be held by someone else.

You had your chance with the most honest version of me, the one who loved without calculation, who showed up without being asked, who kept believing even when it hurt. And losing me was never about one moment. It was about all the little ways you made me feel invisible while I was standing right in front of you.

You taught me to stop offering myself in pieces.

You taught me that not everyone who reaches for you intends to hold you gently.

You taught me that some people love the idea of you, but not the reality of who you are when you stop apologizing for it.

So no.

You don't get to come back.

You don't get to rewrite a story you once abandoned.

You don't get to ask for a second chance at something you didn't try to protect the first time.

And maybe you never will.

Because the version of me who waited, who hoped, who softened she's gone.

In her place stands someone who no longer mistakes love for pain.

Who no longer says "yes" to what once made her feel like she wasn't enough.

Some things don't deserve a second chance.

And that is not bitterness.

It's clarity.

It's self-respect.

It's healing.

It's finally knowing the difference between a lesson and a lifetime.

Chapter 29: It Didn't End with You, It Began with Me

For the longest time, I saw you as the ending. The closing scene. The final full stop in a story that once felt like everything. When you left, it felt like the whole book had collapsed. I thought that losing you was the conclusion of something beautiful, something I might never experience again.

But I was wrong.

Losing you wasn't the end. It was the beginning.

Because something shifted in me after you were gone, something I didn't even know needed to shift. Without you, there was nothing left to distract me from myself. No one to give my love to in hopes of being enough. No story to lose myself in. There was just silence… and me.

And that was where it began.

It began the first time I looked in the mirror and saw someone I didn't recognize, not because I was broken, but because I had spent so long being a version of myself molded by the need to be loved. I realized I had edited myself around you. Softened what needed to be said. Dimmed the parts that shone too brightly. I made myself small so I wouldn't be "too much." But that wasn't love. That was fear.

You were never the ending. You were the mirror I had to look into. The reflection that forced me to confront how easily I abandoned myself just to be chosen.

It didn't end with you because I didn't end.

I slowly began piecing myself back together, not to become who I was before you, but to become someone I had never let myself be. Stronger. Clearer. Louder where I used to be quiet. Still soft, but no longer silent.

I learned to enjoy my own company, not out of necessity, but out of love. I started asking myself what I needed, what I wanted, what I believed. I started living for the moments that made me feel alive, not the ones I hoped would impress you.

And the more I showed up for myself, the less I looked back for you.

I stopped romanticizing what we had. I stopped rewriting the past to make it gentler than it was. I began to see the cracks I used to ignore. The emotional distance I used to explain away. The way

I shrank, hoping you'd finally say what I was always afraid to ask out loud: Do you really love me, or do you just love being loved?

Now I know the answer. And I no longer need to hear it.

Because I am no longer standing at the edge of your absence, waiting for you to return. I am walking in the direction of my own becoming and that path never really started until you left.

So no, the story didn't end with you.

It began with me

The day I chose not to chase,

The day I stopped proving my worth,

The day I picked myself over your silence.

That was the beginning.

The real one.

And it's still being written

Page by page, without you.

And beautifully, finally,

without apology.

Chapter 30: Of All the Words I Never Said

Of all the words I never said, it's the quiet ones that stayed the longest. The small truths I buried beneath hesitation. The sentences I rewrote in my mind a hundred times but never let pass through my lips. The confessions I softened, the questions I swallowed, the pain I wrapped in silence because I thought silence would hurt less.

But it didn't.

It just lingered.

It stayed in the pauses between conversations, in the way I smiled when I wanted to cry, in the way I changed the subject when the truth got too close. It stayed in my body, in my chest, in my bones, all those unsaid words becoming weight I never meant to carry.

I didn't say how much it hurt when you started pulling away. I didn't say how deeply I was trying to hold on without looking desperate. I didn't say how tired I was not of loving you, but of trying to love you in ways that didn't erase me.

I didn't say that I saw the distance long before it became obvious. That I noticed the shift in your voice, the colder way you laughed, the replies that felt more like echoes than conversations.

I didn't say that I knew you were leaving before you did. I felt it in the way you looked at me like you were already forgetting. I saw it in the way you started imagining a life where I didn't fit.

I didn't say how much I wanted to be chosen. Not just kept around. Not just tolerated. Not just almost loved.

But I say it now.

Because this chapter, this final chapter is not for you. It's for me.

It's for the person I was when I stayed silent.

For the person who waited for the right moment that never came.

For the one who believed love was measured in sacrifice.

For the one who kept hoping their presence would be loud enough to be heard without speaking.

And it's for the version of me who finally understands that love is not quiet when it matters. That your truth is not a burden. That saying what you feel is not weakness, it's how you stay honest with yourself.

So here they are.

All the words I never said:

I loved you.

I needed more.

I was afraid.

I stayed longer than I should have.

I wanted to be chosen without having to lose myself to be wanted.

I deserved better.

I forgive you.

I forgive me.

And I'm done writing you into every page of my life.

Because this isn't your story anymore.

It's mine.

And I will not end it with silence.

www.ingramcontent.com/pod-product-compliance
Lightning Source LLC
Chambersburg PA
CBHW070116080526
44586CB00013B/1314